Bold Move

Attract Creative Traits

Otensia Dallas

Printed in the United States of America.

Published by

Light
PUBLISHERS

ISBN: 978-1-953759-80-1 (paperback)

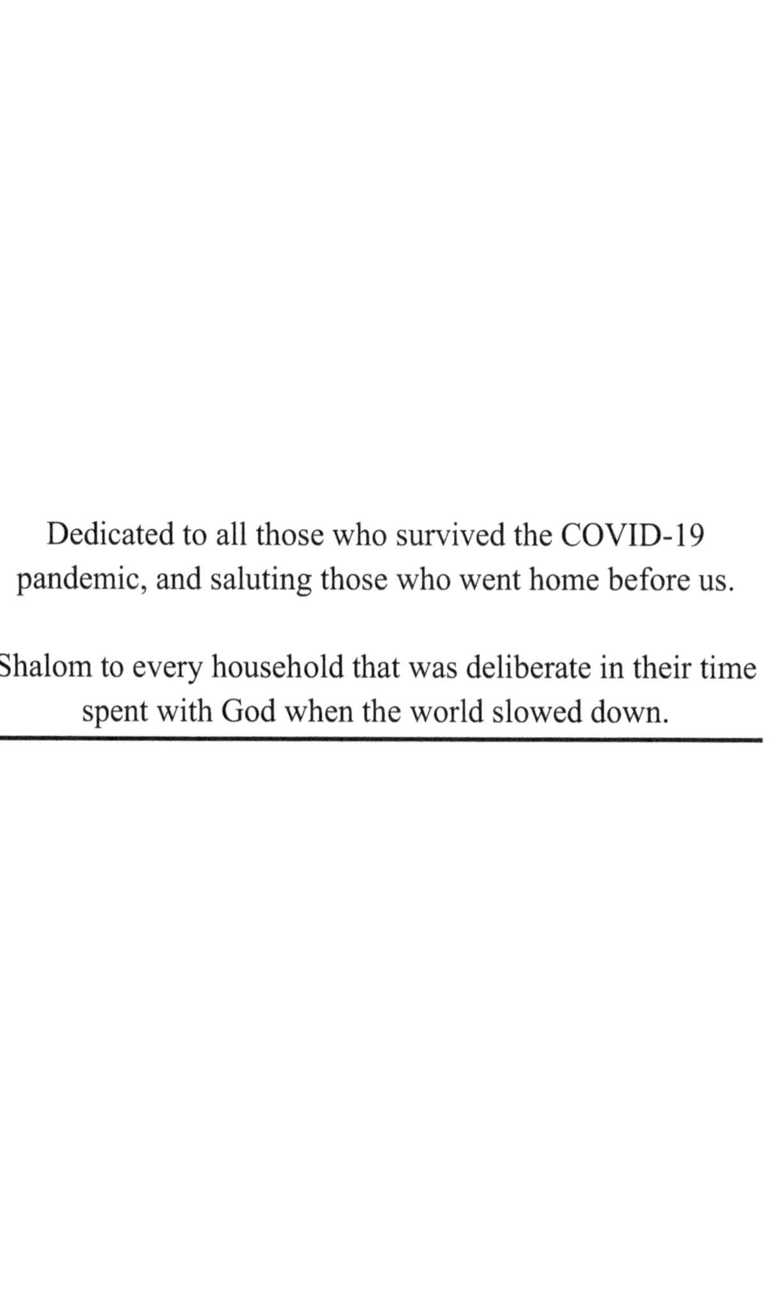

Dedicated to all those who survived the COVID-19 pandemic, and saluting those who went home before us.

Shalom to every household that was deliberate in their time spent with God when the world slowed down.

Acknowledgments

I thank the Lord my saviour for the opportunity to write this devotional, for placing me on a path and telling me which way to go. He uses ordinary things and makes them beautiful. To You, Lord, be the glory.

I am grateful to my family and some of our friends who gathered nightly to pray and share about God's goodness during the shutdown of 2020. Out of this came Bold Move.

A special thanks to my mother, Hyacinth Banton, and my sister, Donna Russell, who started this prayer session before the pandemic and ensure that it continues even now.

Thanks to Yvonne Spence and Althea Chin who partnered with me in prayer for months as we sought God for His plan for our lives.

Thank you to the following people who read my lessons and provided feedback: Tania Barnes, Alecia Speid (sister, friend and prayer warrior), Chrisann Speid, Dr. Douglas Clarke, Karim Swainson, Ann-Marie Graham-Menzie, Karla Black, Trudiann Duncan, Janet Russell, Antoinette Adamson, Claudine Martin, Lesline Burchell and Shane Hall.

Thanks to my pastor, Rev. Cecil B. Stone, who has been patient with me and allowed me room to grow.

To Bishop Derrick Smith, thanks for your support and the opportunities you create for those of us growing in ministry.

To one of my secret weapons, my sis, Gillian Dallas, without whom I would not have gotten to this final stage.

To my publisher, Crystal Daye, and the staff at DayeLight Publishers, thank you for your professionalism and making this process a wonderful adventure.

I'm grateful to all the Bold Movers who listen and share our podcast, Bold Move with Otensia. Thank you for rising with me every weekday morning as we move bold as lions.

Finally, to you, my readers, thank you for picking up this book; it has two partners: your Bible and prayer journal, use them daily.

Table of Contents

Introduction

During the COVID-19 pandemic in 2020, we had a nightly prayer meeting. As we were mostly at home, there were a few issues with schedules so as a family we could all participate. One night, I felt that I should share with the group and that night after we ended, there was a feeling that we should still be on the call. In fact, some people called back. My sister, Gillian, prompted me to share a Bible lesson. I agreed but didn't share with her that it was a confirmation of what I felt I should be doing. The next evening, I shared, then I took Gillian's other advice to ask if people would mind. Sister Janet's response: *When guided by the Holy Spirit, there is no need to seek approval. It is an answer to my prayers. You went to preaching class and it is time for this. Please continue to use the talents entrusted to you.*

On April 24, 2020, I started writing this. *Ministries Alive,* at Springfield Garden United Methodist Church, was on our second reading of "*Draw the Circle: The 40-Day Prayer Challenge*" by Mark Batterson. I decided to read my copy of the book a bit differently. Although I had purchased it in kindle format, I also wanted a hard copy. The first reading started a little over a week before New York City shut down due to COVID-19. I chose not to make notes in my copy then; I knew I would be reading it again. Immediately after completing the first reading, our ministry decided to read it again. This time I took a different approach. As I took notes, I expanded my prayer journal and repeated some readings more than one day so I lagged behind the group in terms of pages, but I needed a bit more out of some lessons. Today, I am on Day 9, right after a *God Idea*, looking at the *Dream Factory*. A few hours later, as I planned the night's lesson, I felt that I should put this together as a formal lesson. There was no name given to me at the time so I was not sure what it would be called. In fact, I saved it in my files as "Family Prayer." I have never been to the Dream Factory but I found a dream there today.

Later, in my bathroom, while reading my affirming statements I use daily, the title popped: ***Bold Move: Attract Creative Traits.*** I had created the phrase "Attract Creative Traits" for the word "act" while doing the video review during a business training session. I wrote it in my quote collections and had it on my bathroom wall to remind myself of the power of acting: moving. I never thought it would be part of the basis of one of my books, but I have come to realize that as you act, you really attract creative traits.

I pray that the simplicity of these pages which follow help to deepen people's walk with Christ. Everyone who opens these pages will find God's encouragement to start again, push through, and make it count. God has given us promises on which we can rely. I was deliberate in leaving pieces of the stories out of my lessons.

My hope is to entice you to read for yourself the wonderful Word of God. In them you will find life and that life is hidden in Christ.

Otensia Dallas

Day 1

Anticipation

Lord, I open my heart to You today. Help me to see that You are doing a new thing among us. As I dedicate this time to You, Lord, please consecrate me anew and prepare me for Your great thing. Thank You, Abba.

Baseline: 2 Kings 3:15-17

Joshua 3:5 (ESV) – Then Joshua said to the people, "Consecrate yourselves, for tomorrow the Lord will do wonders among you."

Having anticipation or "great expectations" can be frustrating at times. This story tells of three kings who were under attack. They decided to be defensive and found their backs against a wall, so to speak. They made the judgment to cross a desert to outwit their enemy but underestimated and paid a great price, or would have, if God had not intervened. As they were crossing the desert, they ran out of water. Imagine three large armies with people and animals and no water. The enemy—the

Moabites—knew where this assemble was but they were well rested and had enough water to quench their thirst.

This is similar to when we make our plans and come up against situations that are so unexpected and seemingly impossible that the best minds cannot think of a solution. God always has the answer and if we can trust Him, we will be more than conquerors.

The kings came to Elisha, but the prophet was mad. He only regarded King Jehoshaphat and told the King of Israel that he would not even regard him otherwise. Why would the prophet speak to people in distress in this manner? The king of Israel was the child of Ahab and Jezebel, people who had killed the prophets of God. The other King of Edom represented the descendants of Esau, who had refused to help Jacob's descendants, Israel, on their way to the Promised Land. Being in the right company is important. Sometimes our lives are not right before God but being among the righteous who pray fervently can cause us to prevail. Yet each of us have a part to play.

Here in the desert place, the leaders of the three kingdoms came to seek knowledge from the man of God. The prophet did something that seemed strange; he called for the musicians. As the musicians played, God ministered to him and he prophesied. And he said, Thus saith the Lord, Make the valley full of ditches. For thus saith the Lord, Ye shall not see wind, neither shall ye see rain; yet the valley shall be filled with water, that ye may drink, both ye, and your cattle, and your beasts. (2 Kings 3: 16-17 - KJV). Not only did God fill the ditches with the water they asked for, but He also gave them their enemies and cities into their hands. He also used His glory to trap the enemy. The Moabites looked at what God had done and made their own interpretation. The sun shining on the water looked like blood. In their limited understanding, they could not comprehend that God made water in the desert place. They went to devour but were devoured instead.

Today, we need to move in anticipation, let the music of our praise, singing and prayer rise to God. Listening for His instructions may seem foolish, and it may take much effort to dig ditches, but work at something even when you cannot see how it will bring the desired result. You cannot outdo what God does. When your enemy sees the results, they will come to devour but God has laid them in your hands. The enemy of fear will see your plan and tell you that you cannot, only to realize that the blueprint is already on its way to the construction company, and you will be able to bring that dream-building into existence.

We know that eyes have not seen, ears have not heard neither have we thought of the things that God has planned for those who love the Lord and are called according to His purpose (see 1 Corinthians 2:9-10).

Attract Creative Trait

What you anticipate will show in what you do, not what you say.

1. Analyze what your actions say to you.

2. Create an annotated calendar with the outline of the project you are working on and those you consider completing.

3. Set goals for each day to get you to an excellent finish.

4. Make allowances for detours and stretch yourself.

5. Ask the experts for advice and when you get it, do it.

Song:
"Hall of Fame" by The Script

Watch:
darrendaily.com

Lord, thank You for reminding me that I cannot outwork or outthink You. You told us that Your ways and thoughts are higher than ours. As I work on my project, no matter how daunting the task, help me, Father, to rely on You with thanksgiving and praise. I know if I dig the ditches, You will fill them with water. Thank You that I continue to attract creative traits, in Jesus' Name and for God's Sake. Amen.

(Hear + Do) Pray = Life

Note to Self

Day 2

Be Relentless

Lord, thank You for giving me dreams and sometimes problems that force me to keep pushing. Help me to see things through to the end. As I start my race, I know it is as important to finish it. Thank You, Abba, for Your relentless pursuit of Your plans for us.

Baseline: Matthew 7:7-8

Here in Matthew 7:7-8, we see the power of seeking, especially being relentless about what we want to acquire. Sometimes we are not sure if what we are seeking is the right thing, but in Matthew 6:33 we are told how to seek. We must seek out the kingdom of God and His righteousness. If we put getting to know God first, then He promises that all that we need will be added to us. This means that in all we do, God has to take first place. So, we give Him our mornings.

I have come to learn that morning does not only mean the time of day but the first part of everything we do. It would require us to acknowledge Him first before we start our conversations or conduct our activities. Ask for His directions and be willing to be obedient. Seek, connotes to actively look for; focused and intentional. Isaiah 55:6 encourages us to seek the Lord while He is near which suggests that there are times when we may not be able to find God. I know that has nothing to do with Him because He is omnipresent—He is everywhere. So why does the prophet specifically encourage us about when to seek God?

The Spirit does not always strive with man (see Genesis 6:3), so while we are fresh before we become entangled in situations, we must make deliberate actions to seek God. We want to make sure that what we are about to undertake is part of God's will for our lives. You may have already started but you can make it a new day by changing your thoughts and actions. Start your new morning of asking God to help you make the right changes to get you in the place you are supposed to be.

I end with this story of an African American man and a humble-looking seed. As I read "Draw the Circle," I was reminded of George Washington Carver who actively sought God in the mornings. He asked about the peanut and God gave him an answer. There are so many products that came from this man seeking God, literally in the morning: one is my favorite: the peanut butter.

So, what are we really seeking God for? It is that His kingdom will come on earth and His will be done (see Matthew 6:10). Furthermore, Matthew 13:44-46 tells us that the kingdom of God is like a man who finds a precious stone in a field. He puts it back, goes, and sells all that he has to buy the field. How precious and what risk sweetly rewarded? How will you start your mornings if you know that spending time actively seeking answers from God will revolutionize the things that you do?

I started walking every morning. It is an exercise I have enjoyed since childhood and often use it to clear my mind. During this season, however, it took on a new meaning. It became one of the times I actively sought God. As I walked, we talked or rather in the beginning I talked. Little by little I learned to listen, then I learned to see. I knew that God had a message for me, but I had to take the time and consistently, relentlessly seek it out.

Attract Creative Traits

Examine how you engage God. Starting with your mornings, what can you do to invite God to a more intimate space? Get a list of the prayer watches and use the focus to help you seek God in the hour you choose to pray consistently. Keep a prayer/scripture journal. Write your prayer requests and corresponding praise reports. Set time aside (maybe once or twice per year) to review your journal.

Recommended Reading:
"Command Your Morning" by Cindy Trimm

Song:
"Great is Thy Faithfulness" by Chris Rice

Sweet Lord, there is so much I want to do at times, but I do not know where to start. As I begin this dawn, give me the drive to seek You. Change my heart from stone to flesh that I will know and do Your will. Help me to push against the grain of mediocrity and settling for at least. Wake up the giant in me that runs with Your Word that it is possible. All I ask, in Jesus' name and for God's Sake, Amen.

(Hear + Do) Pray = Life

Note to Self

____

____

____

____

____

____

____

____

____

____

____

____

____

____

Day 3

The Power of Prayer and Praise

Today, dear Abba, I begin with praise. I borrow the words from Bethel and exclaim that "my weapon is a melody." Oh Lord, what will I give to You for all the benefits You have given me? I lift up my head and invite You in, mighty King of Glory. Thank You, Abba.

Baseline: Acts 19:1-17

Sometimes you may think that people giving you a well-earned commendation is a good thing when it is far from the truth. In these events, we see Paul and Silas in Macedonia. Paul had a vision and went in obedience to this part of the world. He had been staying in Lydia's house where he was teaching the gospel. There was a young woman following them, Paul and Silas, yelling out that these are men of God. At first, it puzzled me that the men of God would be upset at this free advertising. Then I understood that it was the intentions of the one giving the praise that was important.

We are told to try the spirit in 1 John 4:1-5. Likewise, 1 Corinthians 13:3 helps us to see that it is possible for people to give abundantly for reasons other than love, so we need to be able to discern the spirit. For Paul and Silas, the situation was similar. To acknowledge this young woman's commendations, they would give endorsement to the power of divination that came with it. They were not hungry for praise but desired to teach Christ and His righteousness. So, they rebuked the spirit from this young woman.

The girl's freedom from the powers of divination caused Paul and Silas their personal freedom. They were accused falsely, beaten, and thrown in prison. Many times, fighting for freedom, whether it is our own or for others, whether spiritual or other forms of freedom, may lead to us being in some form of prison. The great thing is that these men were familiar with the power of God so they were praising and praying at midnight. It meant that they were keeping others awake because it is reported that the other prisoners heard them. Here is another form of free advertising, only this time, God gets the praise.

The challenge to us is to pray and praise in our midnight prisons, whatever they may be. As we found out before, morning is not just a time of day; midnight also represents a time period when our backs are against the wall and all options seem to be unavailable. It is that part of life that appears impossible and we are asked to sing God's song in a strange land. It is fighting through the unthinkable. In the end, there will be an earthquake, a change so remarkable that it draws attention.

God answers the persistent in this season. How will you react to the prison you find yourself in, whether self-made or otherwise? Will you defy the situation and dare to praise and pray until there is an earthquake-type move in your life? Put it to the test and experience what only God can do.

Attract Creative Traits

What is the midnight hour that you are experiencing or have just experienced? It may be a target that you have yet to hit or a health challenge, loss of income, or the fate of a loved one. You may be good, but your community needs to change. As you outline that challenge, start praising God for the outcome you desire. Even in the face of what may appear as defeat, pray and praise just the same. You have control over two things; the way you view things and what you do. Prayer and praise are only one part of the work. A plan of action is needed; even God used the formula of working six days and resting on the seventh. Now go after it. MOVE!

Recommended Reading:

"Draw the Circle" by Mark Batterson

Father, only You can work against what tries to make us be less than we should. You bring about great victories. I dedicate every aspect of my life to You. You have a track record that clearly proves to me that You can handle anything that comes my way. Lord, lead me in a plain path, and in my midnight season, remind me of Your songs. Teach me to pray now so that I will know how to pray and praise then. More than all, Lord, keep me always hungry and thirsty for You so I will only have room for You, in Jesus' name and for God's sake I pray. Amen.

(Hear + Do) Pray = Life

Note to Self

Day 4

Focus

Abba, thank You. Many times, I look around and wonder if I heard You correctly because of what my eyes see. Lead me in the path where I hear You always. Open my understanding today as I spend time in the life of Your prophet, Elijah, knowing that You are no respecter of persons and what You have done in his life, you can do for each of us as well. Thank You, Abba.

Baseline: 1 Kings 18:41-46

Elijah was a mighty prophet who was passionate about serving God. He lived in a time when the rule of the land had put the one true God aside and worshipped other gods. These traditions were introduced through intermarriages with other cultures. God had warned the children of Israel about this. Today, it is not so much the physical intermarriages that are important as the spiritual ones. The Word asks, how can two walk unless they agree? (See Amos 3:3). It is important to align yourself with people who share your values and, more than all, have the same belief about your God. This includes how they treat other people and the values they place on human lives.

Elijah prayed and it didn't rain for three and a half years. He had just called on the God who answered by fire, and He accepted his offering. Elijah killed the prophets of Baal in honor of his God, the mighty defender. He now gave his prophetic word to the king that he should hurry home as there is rain coming (see I King 18:44). It is important to note that the king understood that Elijah was not making idle talk. He had demonstrated that he was in communication with God.

The interesting fact is that Elijah heard rain before there was any evidence of rain. What we hear is very important, therefore we must protect our ear gate. The Word states in Romans 10:17 that faith comes by hearing. What and who we listen to will impact what we do, say, and become. We will notice that only Elijah heard the abundance of rain, but he didn't let not seeing it sway him. There are times when God will speak to just you and others may not understand. In those moments, you must be sure of your relationship with God. Focus on what He tells you, even when everything looks like the opposite of what you heard.

Elijah sent his servant to look toward the sea for the rain cloud. The servant came back puzzled, stating that he did not see anything. I am wondering why Elijah didn't go to see for himself. I suppose he didn't want the natural vision to mess with the faith he had obtained through hearing the Word of

God. Too often God tells us something, but because we look around and do not see it, we start to doubt and lose focus.

While Elijah needed the fruit of his words to appear, he placed his focus on God. I wonder who among us would be willing to go six times to develop a dream God gave us, when each time we see no evidence of it coming true? Would you look at the thing before your eyes or would you believe what was spoken to you? Elijah placed his head between his knees, maybe in an attempt to protect the Word. He was willing to endure getting bad news repeatedly about the thing he had professed publicly. He was willing to keep his focus on what he heard—abundance of rain—and stayed steady in prayer.

Attract Creative Traits

Identify what causes you to be distracted from your goals. Make preparations for those distractions. Eliminate those that you can and limit the others. For example, set a time limit for the length of your conversations, share your goals with the people your actions will impact, and outline boundaries (make sure you stick with them). Only fill your calendar with activities that will enhance your goal, and, by the way, **fill** your calendar.

Recommended Readings:

The Secret by Rhonda Byrne

Mind Power Into the 21st Century Techniques to Harness the Astounding Powers of Thought by John Kehoe

Lord, thank You for a faith that helps me stay focused on You and Your plans for me. I ask for Your help when my eyes look for the answers that You have promised, and they do not yet appear in the physical. I keep my head down and press into You with the activities that produce my rain. I know You have ordained my blessing in the presence of my enemies, and I already have the victory. I trust You, Lord, and keep Your Word as my guide even while I endure less than desirable news. I know if I continue to seek You, in due time, that small fist-size cloud will soon pour out an abundance of rain. Thank you, Lord, in Jesus' name and for God's sake. Amen.

(Hear + Do) Pray = Life

Note to Self

____

____

____

____

____

____

____

____

____

Day 5

Everyday Life

Abba, thank You that I am fearfully and wonderfully made. I dedicate all that I am to You today, my walking, talking and everyday life. May Your light shine through me in all I do. Thank You, Abba.

Baseline: Romans 12:1-2

In my reading today, the author spoke about being consecrated to God, which means to be set apart for special service. Many times we think of being set apart as being placed on a shelf for a special occasion or event, for example, Christmas curtains and towels set aside for visitors. While I do understand why people may leave those items for special times and events, God does not want us to be out of touch or out of reach on a top shelf. What He desires from us is to have our lives in service for Him, completely dedicated to Him. *How can You use my hands, Lord?*

There was a particular time when I had to work with someone who was very spiteful. It was difficult to endure until I remembered that my work must please God. I started focusing on how I could serve God all the time on my job, and He turned the situation around. Giving God our all may seem a bit much, after all, some believe that we need some time to express ourselves. Our truest self-expression, however, comes when we are sold out for God. He gives you grace in those tough situations that only you can handle. Some of these issues would break other people to the point of unrecognition, but they build you.

If we imagine that every action we take is aimed to please God, we will act a little differently at times. We would be much more pleasant when we say good morning to our neighbors, even the ones with nasty attitudes. It would show up in the way we correct our children, regard adults, and complete even simple tasks. If we knew that God wants to be pleased with our attitude in everyday things, such as eating our food, we would express more gratitude rather than complain when we have to eat the same thing two days in a row. It may not seem like we are doing much by doing the simple things, but consider that our everyday lives reflect our true lives and, therefore, must reflect the one we say we truly love.

Here's a challenge for all of us. Here's what Paul wants us to do, God helping us:

> Take our everyday, ordinary life—our sleeping, eating, going to work, and walking around life—and place it before God as an offering. Embracing what God does for us is the best thing we can do for Him.

Don't become so well adjusted to our culture that we fit in without thinking. Instead, fix our attention on God—we'd be changed from the inside out. Readily recognize what He wants from us and quickly respond to it. Unlike the culture around us, always dragging us down to its level of immaturity, God brings the best out of us and develops well-formed maturity in us.

Read:
Romans 12:1-2 (The Message)

Attract Creative Traits

Identify five ways you can be deliberate about pleasing God in your everyday activities. If you already do these things, fish out five other ways to add to them. Next, decide on one that you will begin or improve on today.

Website:
proverbs31.org

Recommended Readings:
The Threshing Floor by Juanita Bynum

What to Say When You Talk to Yourself by Shad Helmstetter

Make Today Count by John Maxwell

Father, humbly I present myself to You as a living sacrifice. I recognize that I'm not really my own but wholly belong to You. Help me to always remember that when I do anything, it should be done to Your glory. Forgive me, Lord, when I forget, and help each of us to forgive each other as well. We desire to be well-rounded and mature in You, so help us to rise above the culture of society, family, and religion. This we pray, in Jesus' Name and for God's sake. Amen.

(Hear + Do) Pray = Life

Note to Self

____

____

____

____

____

____

____

____

____

____

____

____

____

____

Day 6

What Does it Mean to Pray Through?

Abba, thank You for teaching me the joy of being persistent. So many times, I've wanted to throw in the towel, but You reminded me of the vision that You have set before me and gave me the drive to press on. With such a grateful heart, I say thank You, Lord.

Baseline: Matthew 15:21-28

Have you ever had a situation where no matter how you pray it seems to stay the same way? My family and I have endured years of one of us being constantly ill. At times it seems as if our prayers for complete healing will not be answered. I looked at the scriptures and found a story of a woman who came to Jesus because her daughter was ill. She was first discriminated against by the disciples: the ones who had experienced Christ's healing of blind men, boys with demons, and raising the dead. This woman did not belong to the same faith or culture as Jesus and His disciples. She was a foreigner and considered of less importance to the Jewish people.

The insult of the disciples paled in comparison to the ones she received from Christ. First, He ignored her, He didn't even respond to her pleas. She was determined like the children we often think less of and, in faith, she continued to press through. I want us to consider the things for which we need healing. It may be personal or, like this woman, attached to us. The important thing is to press through no matter what. As if ignoring her wasn't enough, Jesus called her a dog. He said, "It is not right to take the children's bread and throw it to the dog?" (Matthew 15:26 - ESV). To many of us, this would have created such a fight—we would have forgotten why we came.

The woman was so focused on her needs that I believe she came determined to find her answer in anything Jesus said or did, even in comments others may see as insults. She knew the Word so when He spoke her language, she was able to answer. She quickly realized that if healing was in the bread that the children received, then the crumb presented to the dogs had the same ingredients and was willing to take the scraps from the master's table. With her persistence, she was able to receive healing for her daughter.

The questions for us becomes: What are we willing to endure to get the answer from God? Do we want the instant "take care of it this moment" answer? Or are we willing to tarry and press through the silence, the answer which seems to overlook us and press into Him for life-changing experiences? Do our souls pant, thirst, ache, and will not rest until we drink of the everlasting water? This woman knew that worshipping unlocked the door, crying aloud gets us an audience, and faith brings us our healing. Will we be like this Canaanite woman, seeking even the scraps from the master's table?

Attract Creative Traits

Revisit an activity for which you did not have the desired outcome. Identify the things you did well. Examine what made them successful. Analyze how you can integrate those actions or similar ones in what you are doing today. Next, identify what you need to improve. Analyze the changes you have to make and start using them immediately. I loved the terms Cortney Jackson-Harris used: "glows" for the successful things and "grows" to help her students make similar self-assessments. Know what will get you where you need to be, and eliminate or grow yourself out of the habits and traits that make you come in second.

Recommended Readings:

TNT The Power Within You by Claude Bristol and Harold Sherman

The Art of War by Cindy Trimm

The Book of Esther - The Bible

Father, I bless You for allowing us a glimpse into this woman's life. Like the scrap that she was willing to take from the master's table, we see just a small part of her faith and apply it to our lives. Lord, I believe You when you say,

Let the weak say I am strong and let the poor say I am rich. With this faith, I declare over my life that I am made whole. I may not see it now, but I know as I head back to that thing that seems so stubborn, all is well and healing has taken place. So, I worship You, Lord, knowing that Your Word accomplishes all that it sets out to do. I hear You, Lord, and live by faith. With praise, I say thank You, Lord, in Jesus' Name and for God's sake. Amen.

(Hear + Do) Pray = Life

Note to Self

____

____

____

____

____

____

____

____

____

____

____

____

____

____

Day 7

John the Revelator

Abba, thank You for Your divine will in our lives. Thank You for giving us revelations, sometimes through dreams and visions, and through others You have placed in our lives. I thank You, God, that if we are willing, You will show us how and what to do. With a grateful heart, I say thank You for these mercies.

Baseline: Revelation 4:11:

"Thou art worthy, O Lord, to receive glory and honor and power: for thou hast created all things, and for thy pleasure they are and were created." (KJV).

John, the disciple whom Jesus loved, had a revelation while on Patmos. The book of Revelation is so out of the ordinary that I could not reconcile with the fact that Patmos is an actual place in Greece. During his time in exile, John had visions that he recorded in this book.

In Chapter 4, there is much activity taking place in the heavens. John was looking up as he was "caught up" in the

Spirit. It was loud and filled with activities; it was also beautiful. Things that we clamor for was second place. John gave an image of 24 elders falling down before the throne of God in worship. Three observations can be made about this activity:

1. They fell down before the One who was seated.

A throne is a place of authority, therefore, they had to be lower than the one in authority. Falling down is not just a physical act but it is also a position of the heart—an attitude of submission. God needs to know that when He has given us authority that we treat it as a place of service, first to Him and then to the people we are called to serve. He gives grace to the humble (see James 4:6).

2. They cast their crowns down.

Crowns show the honor of the ones who wear them. They represent prestige, and the people who wear crowns usually regard each other as equals. Here the beautiful things that represent status were thrown down, symbolizing that they were in the presence of one with whom they were not equal. I also believe that this action represents their willingness to discard the things we think we need to give us recognition. Before the throne, the only one who is exalted is the one sitting on the throne.

3. They acknowledged who God is.

He is worthy to receive glory and honor. The Word says that every tongue will confess that He is Lord (see Philippians 2:10). Putting your voice in the atmosphere enables you to reach the throne, and worship carries you there quickly.

Finally, they acknowledged why we and all creation were made, and that is for God's pleasure. Simply stating: "my stubborn will at last I've yielded. I will be Thine and Thine alone." ~ Amy Grant

Attract Creative Trait

Praise and worship do wonders! They bring us into God's presence. Today's activity is about employing these two powerful resources. This may be your strong area, or you may be learning how to get here. You may start with the Psalms. Personalize them, place yourself in these lines as you "sing" them to the Lord. Here's an example using Psalm 21:1-2:

I will joy in thy strength, O Lord: and in thy salvation how greatly shall I rejoice. Thou hast given me my heart's desire and have not withholden the request of my lips.

As you spend time praising, it is important to transition to worship. This is where you exalt God for who He is, not for what He has given you or what you want. Bless His great name, raise your hand, and dance before Him. There are many worship leaders who can help you here, but remember, He loves to hear from you.

Recommended Reading:

The Psalms

Listen to (these are some of my current favorites):
Sinach, Elevation Worship, Hillsong, Bethel, Tasha Cobbs, Miranda Curtis

Do:

Sing your own song to the Lord—tune and rhythm do not matter.

Father, the things I have gathered pale in comparison to what You have planned for me. Help us to remember that You spoke and the world was formed. While some scientists work to disprove this, I know that everything that comes about was first formed in the spiritual realm before the natural. Therefore, I cast down the things that I thought were precious before for You. I lay prostrate at Your feet and cry holy, holy holy! Thank You for hearing, Lord, and showing us Your glory, in Jesus' Name and for God's sake. Amen.

(Hear + Do) Pray = Life

Note to Self

____

____

____

____

Day 8

Hidden Legacy

Abba, as I move in faith, I don't know all that You have planned for me. I pray, however, that the works of my hands please You and that You bless them. You declare that a good man leaves an inheritance for his children's children. Like your daughter, Ruth, I work to provide for those You have blessed me to take care of. Prosper these hands, Lord, as I bless Your name, Great Jehovah.

Baseline: ***Ruth 4:14:***

"And the women said unto Naomi, Blessed be the Lord, which hath not left thee this day without a kinsman, that his name may be famous in Israel." (KJV).

Ruth 4:21-22 – "And Salmon begat Boaz, and Boaz begat Obed, and Obed begat Jesse, and Jesse begat David." (KJV).

This story is told of Ruth and Naomi. It started out in a time of hardship. I am not sure how long the famine they tried to escape lasted but I know Naomi had about ten years of unfortunate events in her life. Famine forced her to move from her homeland, and death left her bitter. She felt that God had dealt her a hard hand. We can tell, however, that her life was an example to Ruth. In Ruth 1:16, Ruth emphatically said that Naomi's God would be her God. So, we can conclude that she must have learned about this God whom Elimelech and Naomi served. It shows that the life we live is a witness of God to others.

Returning home was bittersweet for Naomi. She still had some property but, based on customs, it wasn't working much to her advantage. They faced another kind of hardship, another famine, although in the midst of plenty. It was the height of the barley harvest. But in the house, there was a lack until one person made a decision to go against the grain. Ruth was an immigrant, and we don't know what skills she had but she decided to get a lowly job that put food on the table. Her actions throughout the story showed persistence and great courage. She was willing to leave home and all that she knew. This created opportunities for her. People admired her and her actions toward her mother-in-law. Her name went ahead of her, so when she came into the place of opportunity, people knew of her and her reputation of being courageous.

God favored Ruth even on the first day that she went out. She went to the field of the person who could take care of the other issues that plagued the household. Not only did he give her more than she would have had elsewhere, he placed his protection over her head. The bravest part of this story to me is Ruth going to the threshing floor. She went totally on the advice of her mother-in-law. Her acts of obedience in this situation demonstrated her willingness to be submissive to the one who had the answer.

There must have been some element of risk for her being at the threshing floor; Naomi advised her to be attractive—get in the role for what you want. This is important because many times we want something but no one looking at us could even guess that we are after that thing. Next, her mother-in-law told her to be discreet. Not everyone needs to know your business; they may see you moving but time will reveal what you are truly about. Due to her obedience and willingness to persist, great honor came to Ruth's name, the great-grandmother of David, the giant slayer.

Attract Creative Traits

On the inside is an awesome legacy waiting to be born. Analyze what is one action you need to change that will positively impact generations to come. Analyze areas of your life and challenge yourself to make positive adjustments. Even if things are going well, consider how they would be greater if you made a change. As always, be prayerful in what you do.

Recommended Readings:

The Alchemist by Paulo Coelho

The Magic of Believing by Claude Bristol

Poem:

To Trust by Otensia Dallas

Lord, thank You for hiding things in our hearts and giving us the opportunities to search them out. As we work in our daily lives and encounter challenges, we desire Your help and a relationship with You to tell us which way to go. How do we move? How do we come into a place of refreshing? What are You bringing out of us, Lord? Let us persist for Your Glory, in Jesus' name and for God's sake. Amen.

(Hear + Do) Pray = Life

Note to Self

____

____

____

____

____

____

____

____

____

____

____

____

____

Day 9

Forgiveness Frees Us

Abba, thank You that You paid for our redemption on the cross. As we forgive others their debts, Lord, please forgive us our trespasses. We want to live free, pure lives before You, so search our hearts, Lord, and make them clean. Thank You, Father.

Baseline: Psalm 32:1-11

Each of us has had something that confines us. It may be a situation that seemed to have your hands tied or an illness that immobilized you. Most of us, however, have a different kind of imprisonment, usually in our minds. People fear the unknown, the unfamiliar, and many people hold on to grudges and slights whether real or imagined. In this Psalm, attributed to David, there is rejoicing because of a release through forgiveness. David explains that the person whose sins are covered is "blessed." The story of his sin with Bathsheba is widely told, and most of us would prefer for our stories with that particular shade to be hidden. While I am sure David would have preferred to have this part of this life excluded from the scriptures, I am sure God places them there for a reason. It is not if we will falter, it is what will be our posture when we do. Psalm 32:5 tells how David "acknowledged his sin" and did not hide his iniquity from God. As he confessed to God, he got the release he so needed.

Why do we need to repair the breach that is broken because of sin? Why do we need to humbly ask God for forgiveness? It places us in a place of divine protection—a sweet, secure hiding place kept safe from trouble. We can tell that David finds and fears God. He records the talk with God: "I will instruct thee and teach thee in the way which thou shalt go: I will guide thee with mine eye." (Psalm 32:8 – KJV). The person who trusts in the Lord will have a hedge around them. Not only that, it keeps them out of the reach of the devil, but it also stops them from going into territories they should not even consider.

This calls for rejoicing. Paul asks, What shall we then say? Shall we continue in sin, that grace may abound? (Romans 6:1 - ASV). Not at all. Not when the benefits of being a friend of God are so overwhelmingly amazing. Let each of us examine where we are not walking in forgiveness. It may be unconfessed sins, unforgiveness of self or others. In what other areas of lack of freedom do we operate? Hurry up and find it in Christ, the true life-giver and protector. Memorize His Word and keep them close to your lips.

1. Identify an area where you need to make changes in order to be free. What scriptures can you find to help you pray about this? What actions can you take to make a practical change in this area?

2. What things do you recognize in another person for which you can effectively pray and ask for his/her freedom? Explain how praying for him/her helps you in your walk with Christ.

Recommended Reading:

The Secret Power of Speaking God's Word by Joyce Meyer

Father, thank You for Your forgiveness. You search the heart and know our thoughts afar off. Cleanse me with hyssop and I will be clean. With Your help, I forgive quickly and with joyous abundance. Before I offer my gifts, Lord, You reveal my offense and show me how to make it right. Lord, I am nothing without You—only a human—and neither are my brothers and sisters. We hurt each other oftentimes without intent, and even when intentional, give us the grace to forgive. Keep us in Your will. I pray for God's sake, in Jesus' Name. Amen.

(Hear + Do) Pray = Life

Note to Self

Day 10

Though Trouble Rise (God's Heart)

Abba, thank You, Lord. Once again, I have escaped the trap of the enemy. You cloaked me in disguise, and I have escaped with my soul. They opened their mouths to say aha, but they are confounded. They look with eyes that do not see and with dull ears they try to perceive my path. Thank You, Lord, my way of escape.

Baseline: 1 Samuel 21

David is on the run! He has a powerful man against him, yet he knows that he is innocent. Even in distress, he runs to the House of God—the Lord is his first defense. In speaking to the priest, David was sure not to speak more about his woes and the fact that he was in the process of leaving his country because of his king. He rather used the situation as an opportunity to win.

Some people will look at this story and use less than admirable descriptions for David; others would see the wisdom of God working in this situation. I refuse to put a label on the man of God, but many times I try to figure out what I would have done in the same situation. David spoke his truth to the priest. He related that he was on a mission for the king. We do not know which king was at the forefront of David's mind. Was it Saul or himself, as he was already appointed? Or was it the King of kings? When situations face you, you have the right to decide for yourself what they mean to you. When you speak your truth, do not look to anyone for validation, you do not need to argue or explain. It does not matter what others say, believe or think, that is just their business. What do you think? What do you know about you that is true?

At the temple, David received two things: bread and a sword. Both items are symbols in the Bible for the Word of God. Jesus, when tempted by the enemy, used the Word to counteract him. He made it clear that the Word of God was bread, and while the conversation started with physical hunger, Jesus related that the Word is more sustaining than the natural bread. He established that sustenance is coming from what God says. Eat up the Word of God. Let it be like sweet honey to you (see Psalm 119:103). The priest took the bread from the altar, and there were certain conditions attached to eating it. The same is true of the Word of God. In it we think we find life (see John 5:39). If we study the Word, we will not be ashamed when it is time to use it, and even when we least expect it, God will reveal to us what to say.

The next item was the sword. This was no ordinary sword. It was the one that sealed David's first public victory: Goliath's sword. This is where we can see David's excitement. He did not ask, but said to the priest, "…give it to me." (1 Samuel 21:9 - NIV). He knew this sword as he had used it before. Like the bread, it was in the holy place. It was wrapped in the ephod. The ephod was a piece of accessory which the priest wore, and it carried Urim and Thummim. The priest would inquire of the Lord using this set of materials. Why was Goliath's sword wrapped up in the ephod of the priest? The thing that brings victory is wrapped up in the thing that brings answers from the Lord. Paul refers to the sword of the Spirit as the Word of God. It is in using the Word as a weapon of offense or defense that one is able to gain victory over the enemy.

Armed with these two items, David made his way to Achish, the king of Gath, an enemy of his people. It seems as if when some of these powerful men run from the enemy, whether it is man or nature, they end up under another king's covering: Abraham, Isaac, and now David. David is trying to escape, and we can tell he hopes to go unrecognized, but when God's truth is on you, it is hard to hide. However, the truth in the wrong hands can cause serious damage. Knowing where he was and what was at stake, David quickly assumed another personality so he could escape with his life. This leads to the question each of us must ask ourselves: What about our personalities are we willing to change so we can escape with our very lives?

Attract Creative Traits

1. Choose to see things in the light that brings glory to God and moves you in a positive direction. The negative side is also yours to choose, and both have consequences.

2. Use the Word of God as your sustenance and defense. Find scriptures that speak to your situation and use them as a guide.

3. Consider how the people around you use the truths about you and your circumstances. Discern if it serves your life's purpose or not.

Songs:

He Knows My Name and There's A Healing In This Room With My Name On It by Tasha Cobb Leonard

I Love The Lord by Whitney Houston

Recommended Readings:

The Purpose Driven Life by Rick Warren

Pilgrim's Progress by John Bunyan

Poem:

Name by Otensia Dallas

Father, You know me, and You have set my name before You. As I run like David and Joseph to escape, provide a way out. Your Word, Lord, You have prepared for me as a sword. It cuts into the things that make me fail and fill me up with the healing powers of faith and resistance to the devil. Your answers wrap up that sword that defends me, and when my enemy seeks to overtake me, You give creative disguises to get me on my way. Lord, I look to You. The way before is not clear, but I know I can do this with You. I can persevere, I can live victoriously, I can fulfill my purpose, and I do because You live in me. Thank You, Father, for victory, in Jesus' Name, and for God's sake. Amen.

(Hear + Do) Pray = Life

Note to Self

____

____

____

____

____

____

____

____

____

____

____

Day 11

Naaman's Secret Weapon

Abba, thank You for a secret hiding place. Thank You for a shelter in the time of war. Thank You for giving us victories using unconventional methods. Lord, You are mighty. You confound the wise and give the answers to the babes and suckling. May I always come to You with a clean slate ready to learn. Thank You for doing it again.

Baseline: 2 Kings 5

2 Kings 5:1 - Now Naaman, captain of the host of the king of Syria, was a great man with his master, and honourable, because by him the Lord had given deliverance unto Syria: he was also a mighty man in valour, but he was a leper. (KJV).

Every victory comes with secret weapons. Naaman knew this full well. He was a captain and well trained in war. He had accomplished great victories, yet he had a secret that was a weapon against him. During the COVID-19 pandemic, many people decided not to share with others that they were infected. This is because the virus is highly contagious, and the best way to contain the spread is through social distancing. There are families who had to live segregated lives even within the home to ensure the safety of each person in the household. During this pandemic, there were options. Although millions have been affected, most people had the choice of living safely away from others while having access to medical care. For a leper in Naaman's days, options were limited. Status did not save anyone from banishment.

The protection of the majority of the people was of utmost concern. The leper had to live outside of town without safety measures. They were allowed to come into town but had to stay about sixteen feet from anyone, announcing their presence by yelling out "unclean." Their only reason for coming into town was the "essential service" of getting food. Naaman knew that this was his fate. His household knew his condition and certainly the king of Syria. Why he was given an exception is not clear. Maybe his value to the country allowed him the privilege. What was clear, however, is that his need for healing was urgent.

Being a soldier in an army such as the Syrians, they would go out on what some people call patrol or raids. The nature of Naaman's mission in Israel was not disclosed but when they came back, there was a young girl with Naaman whom they had captured. She worked as the maid for Naaman's wife. Nothing much is told of this little maid, not her name, nor her age, only her role. There are times when God will lead us into obscure positions. We may be captive in a circumstance that may dictate where we are. If we had the choice, many of us would elect to be elsewhere. However, we must understand that wherever we are, we are always in God's service. The decision is for us to be willing to serve every day and always to God and the purpose that He has entrusted to us.

This maid used her knowledge to bring victory to Naaman once more. She used a circumstance that would have caused her to be bitter and made others better. She knew of the power that God had given Elisha. She spoke with her captor. I imagine her saying: "If you were in my country, where this prophet lives, you would be healed." God expects us to sing His praises wherever we go and no matter the circumstances we face. There is no hanging our harps on willow trees, but singing God's songs in strange lands.

We will notice that the maid was not mentioned again in the story. Her part was over. She did what she needed to do. Without her involvement, none of the movements could take place. The story showed that the kings' messages were crossed and poised to bring discord. The bureaucratic paperwork may have gotten in the way, but Naaman's healing was set in motion.

As a secret weapon, you will see others experience pain as they lack the knowledge you have. People cannot understand why you sing praises when things are falling apart around you. They don't understand why you visit that child in prison, why you pray for her and why you call her a mighty woman of God. As a matter of fact, the judge does not know why he is sending her to that special counseling session. That is the beauty of secret weapons; people cannot put their finger on them but they are there.

As Naaman went to Israel this time, he took gifts intended for the person who healed him. He did not take the gifts to the king of Israel but the man of God. We are not told in the story if the maid was thanked or rewarded with any special treatment. After all, she was a secret weapon. Elisha, the prophet, had a secret too: the most high God. Therefore, Elisha refused Naaman's gifts. He knew that the glory belonged to God alone. Naaman also brought back home with him another secret. He declared that he will only offer sacrifices unto the Lord (see 2 Kings 5:17). He also made a request to be pardoned for going to the temple of the other gods when his duties demanded it.

Each of us has a captive situation. Consider your response to and through that circumstance. What is your secret weapon? How are you using it? Where do you place the glory when all is said and done?

Attract Creative Trait

One of the best secret weapons that I have found is prayer. Think of a person or situation outside of your own that needs a remedy. Ask the Holy Spirit to guide you in praying for that person or situation. Pray only what He has instructed you to pray, and see God work. It may not be immediate but there will be evidence when the release has taken place. Be mindful that you give God all the glory and take none for yourself.

Recommended Readings:

The Secret by Rhonda Byrne

Abundance Now by Lisa Nichols

Hello Tomorrow by Cindy Trimm

The Lifestyle of a Watchman by James Goll

Songs:

Search Me Oh God by Cathedral Quartet

The Winds And Waves Know His Name by Bethel Music

Lord, You have been our help in ages past. What an awesome secret weapon! Although You have made Your presence in our lives public, we don't always see You. We bring our gifts, but You do not need them. You said You do not desire sacrifices but a broken and contrite heart. You desire truth in the inward parts. Your Word, Lord, we hide in our hearts; it is secure there and when we need it, it is right there. We hear You over our shoulders, saying, Go this way and not that way. You send us to Jordan to wash and even on the sixth time there seems to be no change but give us the courage to do it one more time. Like Elijah's servant, we will see the fist of a cloud that tells us that the rain has come. Thank You, Lord, that I have seed in the ground. For our secret weapons of warfare, we thank You, Lord, in Jesus' name and for God's sake. Amen.

(Hear + Do) Pray = Life

Note to Self

Day 12

David Brings The Ark From Obed-Edom (The Comeback)

Abba, Lord, thank You that even when I have lost my way, You show me winning examples. In my effort to do things for You, I sometimes do them without You. Please, Lord, correct me in Your mercies. Help me to humbly get back to the drawing board and layout all my plans according to Your will. Direct my path as only You can. Thank You, Lord.

Baseline: 1 Chronicles 15:1-2

1 Chronicles 15:1 - "And David made him houses in the city of David, and prepared a place for the ark of God, and pitched for it a tent." (KJV).

David was a great man. Most kings had things passed down through generations. David, however, had to fight to obtain what God anointed him for. Consider that you are minding your own business at work, and out of nowhere, someone called you and gave you a position. They gave you the position of CEO, but there are several things not adding up. First of all, there is a current CEO who is not stepping down. Another factor is that you have never run a company and you are not qualified. What is more, you don't even work in the office so you cannot get a glimpse as to how things work. With all of that, you still believe that it is possible as the one giving you the position is the same person who appointed the current CEO. Out of nowhere, the Spirit of God falls on you in front of those who did not even think to invite you to your own promotion. At the end of it all, they send you back to the janitor's closet to continue your work.

This was the story of David. He knew he was appointed king, but we don't see where he went about shouting about what he was. He knew his time was not yet and his family didn't cut him any slack; he had to return to the field to tend to the sheep. David's way to the throne was very hard. He ran for his life, he lived among the enemy of his people, and he had only those who were down and out of luck on his side. At one point, he was in a cave with over 400 men, yet he felt so alone as they were all dependent on him with no one else to share the responsibility. He had one source of strength and that was the presence of God. He often cried out to the Lord and acknowledged that wherever he went, whether it was accidentally or by design, if it was God's will or because he went on his own accord, it was a good place. Even if he made his bed in hell, he knew that God was there. (see Psalm 139:8).

With this in mind, David could not live without the ark of God. He made houses for his large family, and he built a place for the presence of God. God needs to know that when He has established you, you will keep that place that belongs to Him. He does not wish to take over. He wants to know that you voluntarily placed Him in the middle of all that is taking place in your life. It is a place that you have prepared with careful consideration. You prepared a place for God to dwell in your life.

David's zeal sometimes got in his way. He saw the need to get the ark of the Lord back from the enemy's camp, and he did. It takes boldness to go to the enemy and demand your stuff and walk away with it. David was used to being in charge and since no one else had, he felt that the way he handled everything would do for the ark of God. He neglected one part: he did not consult with God on how to get the ark back to the place he had prepared for Him. There are times that we fast, pray and work for the things that are rightly ours, but we fail to ask God how to handle them. Mishandling the things that God has given us can be deadly.

And death is not always physical. Many times, we get overwhelmed because we didn't set up a schedule—there are no measures put in place for the things that were going on before, so that blessing may seem like a curse. While David was angry with God for the death that occurred, God blessed the one whose house received the ark. For three months Obed-Edom's house was blessed; his field, his cattle and the women in his family all bore fruit.

What I love about David is that the moment he realized what must be done, he sprang into action. He must have dedicated time reviewing the history books to realize that the way they had tried to bring the ark back had a flaw. He figured out what had to be done and armed with the accurate information, he put things in place to get the ark back to His dwelling place.

David was a bit extra! Not only did he get the Levites to carry the ark, but he also set up a full celebration of this move. Some things need a whole new team. David had singers, trumpeters and they all lifted up their voices with joy. A whole production made to and for the Lord. That is what He deserves; make your joy full in the Lord. "Rejoice in the Lord always: and again I say, Rejoice." (Philippians 4:4 - KJV). David didn't just ask the people to sing, he dedicated the best to the Lord. Then they sacrificed on the way back to Jerusalem. The Lord was pleased, and He helped them.

1 Chronicles 15:26: "And it came to pass, when God helped the Levities that bare the ark of the covenant of the Lord, that they offered seven bullocks and seven rams." (KJV).

Many times, we expect to bring out God's purpose without God's help. To ensure victory, we must ask Him for the strategies we need to win, and set the plan in motion as we praise and sacrifice. Then God will definitely help.

The following protocol is important—with it comes delegation. Consider a project that you are completing that requires teamwork.

1. Decide who should be on your team. Identify the roles that each person should play.

2. Ensure that they are aware of the part they are expected to play and are prepared.

3. Spend time working out the kinks (measure twice, cut once).

4. Execute.

Recommended Readings:

The Prayer of Jabez by Bruce Wilkerson

You Can Begin Again by Joyce Meyer

Unqualified by Steven Furtick

Songs:

What A Beautiful Name by Hillsong United

This Amazing Grace by Phil Wickham

All Hail The Power Of Jesus Name by Miles Lane

Father, our great Succor, thank You for being our help. Thank You that I can see what You are saying to me and speak when I am reproved. I want to do great things for You, and I want to be valiant; help me to always remember that I can only do this with Your help and endorsement. You have a standard that even the enemy falls in line with. Thank You for teaching me Your precepts. Thank You for teaching me Your ways. What will I render for Your benefit? I will worship You with my whole heart. I will sing Your praises and listen for Your guidance. I wait patiently on You, Lord, and You heard my cry and considered my supplications. Thank You, God, for honoring the works of my hands, in Jesus' name and for God's sake. Amen.

(Hear + Do) Pray = Life

Note to Self

____

____

____

____

____

____

____

____

____

____

Day 13

Jacob Rests At Bethel

Search me, Abba, and know my heart. My bed has been made with tears and groanings. Correct me with Your tender mercies and let the bones that You have broken rejoice. I will take up the cup of salvation as a rendition to all Your benefits. I will teach transgressors Your ways, just please uphold me with Your hand. Thank You, Abba.

Baseline: Genesis 28 & 35

Jacob is on the run, and he has done enough to get his brother angry. Esau and Jacob are rival twins. It started when their mother, Rebecca, was pregnant. The fighting was so intense that she had to go to God for an answer about what was taking place in her body. She knew she had two great men coming from her and that the older would serve the younger.

For some reason Rebecca favored Jacob, and her husband favored Esau, the older twin. This rivalry continued into adulthood, and Rebecca compounded the matter when she created a plot to rob Esau of his blessing. The plan was successful and led to a deadly threat. While Issacs's preference was for Esau, he knew that the best answer for Jacob was to give him an additional blessing and send him away. This time Jacob had to take action by himself.

Jacob is presented as the younger of the twins, but he is a grown adult. Running for his life, he took a rest at a place called Luz. While here, he took a stone for his pillow, and there he got a revelation as he slept. It seems as if revelations about ourselves and our situations come when we are between that proverbial rock and a hard place. It is also at this time that we will learn things about God that may not have been revealed to us before. When the patient is terminally ill, they learn of this healer. In the courtroom, we find a great counselor. When war would tear us apart, we find the Prince of Peace. Yes, we get these revelations in our tough times.

At this place, Jacob dreamt of a place where angels were ascending and descending. God was at the top of the ladder. It seems to me that while we are struggling with the tough things, if we take a moment, step away and rest our minds from trying to concoct the right answers, God will reveal the truth to us. Right there, God proved that he was in the place which Jacob found so difficult. Alone and separated from others, he was able to experience God in a profound way. Sometimes our separation from others may be physically like those in prison or quarantined. You may be facing a spiritual or mental separation in that you are around others, but you cannot articulate how you feel. In that 'night' season, God still gives assurance and the rest needed.

Jacob had the blessing of his father poured out on him at this place. This time it was not from his earthly father who knew how to play favorites but from his Creator who had ordained him to receive a blessing. We can see that Jacob's ways did not disqualify him from receiving the blessing that was his. He still had to live with the consequences of cheating his brother; he could not go home just yet. But God revealed Himself to him while he was trying to escape.

God could have immediately poured out his blessing of restoration on Jacob, but He knew there were valuable lessons he had to learn. One of them being the value of hard work instead of trickery to obtain what he wanted. He had a brilliant mind, but he had to use it in the right manner. He also learned submission. While it was predicted that he would be the stronger of the twins, Jacob later submitted to Esau as a way to gain forgiveness and protect his family.

For over twenty years Jacob was away from home and the place he later named Bethel. He made a promise to God, vowing that if God kept him and allowed him to return home in peace, this place would be called the House of God, and he would give a tenth of all he had to God. Here we can see a change coming over Jacob. He recognized that God is the atmosphere changer, and He is able to do what needs to be done. He didn't leave it all up to God; he decided the role he would play in his deliverance. It was a promise, and God honors kept promises.

Jacob did not calmly return to Bethel. Trouble in his family caused him to run back to the place where he had experienced God. This time God had increased him to a large family. He had much but he also knew that the presence of God was much more powerful. Jacob's second encounter at Bethel forever changed him and an entire nation.

It started one night as he ran from his brother Esau…

Attract Creative Traits

Finding a way to handle the stress in your life is vital to your success.

1. Spending time in prayer and God's presence provides this source. I have said repeatedly, and I will keep saying this: spend time in the Word of God. Pray God's Word back to Him.

2. Seek wise counsel. Ask your mentors questions and be willing to follow their advice. Ask God to send the right people in your life and keep an active eye out expecting them. This may also include professional help, if it is needed.

3. Use a moral compass. Treat people fairly and do what is right.

4. Take a quick step back from the issue to gain another perspective. See it through others' eyes.

Recommended Readings:

How To Make People Like You In 90 Seconds Or Less by Nicholas Bootman

How To Win Friends And Influence People by Dale Carnegie

The Book Of Proverbs ~ The Bible

Make Today Count by John Maxwell

Visit:

arleneantoinette.com
livingprettyhappy.com
lumosity.com

Do:

Go for a walk or biking; volunteer; use your time wisely to attain your dreams; keep an active journal that records and evaluates your thoughts, feelings, and actions.

Father, many of us are undergoing real trying times. They cause us to make decisions that are not always the best for us. You have promised in Your Word that You will never leave us; You will never forsake us. We know that You neither sleep nor slumber so we pray for Your peace that passes all understanding. Help us to use these times as training times. I pray, dear God, that we would seek Justice and love Mercy. That we would treat our neighbor as we would have loved ourselves to be treated. That we seek out wise counsel in every area of our lives: finances, health-

physical and mental, family, and business. When we find ourselves between a rock and a hard place, we will look to You, the author and the finisher of our faith. In the night season, Lord, speak to us, give us a way out while You sustain us through. I know we have a great future before us because Your plans are for our good. Merciful God, teach us to walk worthy of the calling of our vocation, in Jesus' name we pray, and for God's sake. Amen.

(Hear + Do) Pray = Life

Note to Self

____

____

____

____

____

____

____

____

____

____

____

____

____

____

Day 14

You Are Whole

Abba, as I come to You today, I thank You for always hearing me. I'm filled with gratitude for all You have done for me. You have shown me compassion in my weakest hour, and I thank You for teaching me the power of worship. Hear my prayers today. I humbly ask with gratitude. Amen.

Baseline: Luke 17:11-14

The story is told of ten men who had leprosy. Most times, when we read this passage, we go to the lesson told in verses 17-19 and highlight the one leper who returned to give thanks. Gratitude is very important, and I do not make light of this act. We must live our lives in an attitude of gratitude. However, for this session, I want to pay a bit more attention to the other people in the story.

We see Jesus on the move. I love that about Him: always about His Father's business, never idle. He understood purpose. Here He gets interrupted, which is not the only time this has happened. People took the opportunity to reach out to Him, constantly grabbing Him while He was within their reach. There were the friends lowering the man with palsy, the woman with the issue of blood, and blind Bartimaeus interrupting Jesus on His way to somewhere else. The example which fascinates me the most is in Mark 6:45-56. While He was praying in the mountains, His disciples whom He had sent ahead of Him were in trouble on the lake. He went out to them walking on the water and would have walked past them. This grabbed my attention because they were in trouble simply doing what He instructed them to do. When they cried out, He went to their rescue. Likewise, many times we find ourselves in trouble just doing the things that concern us. We cannot understand how something so routine and good could go so badly and often quite quickly. We know, however, that the eyes of the Lord go back and forth across the earth looking for those whose hearts are loyal to Him (see 2 Chronicles 16:9). His purpose here is to show Himself strong on their behalf. When you see Him, lean in and cry out. Grab His attention!

These men outside the village did just that; they cried out for help. Like on many occasions, Jesus' reaction seems strange to us. He told them to go show themselves to the priest. The priest was in the village they could not enter. I also understand that the lepers would show themselves to the priests when they become healed. However, in the middle of their trouble and with no evidence of healing, Jesus says to them go do that thing as if it is all well. As they went, their miracle was made known on the outside. Please note that the miracle didn't happen when they got to the priest. I believe it took place when they cried out.

You must believe that you are whole. You do not need to be perfect; you need to start moving in the direction of your expected end. As you go, your healing will show up. As Jesus was always on the move, we must do the same. Move in your assignment, cry out to God, hear His response and make sure like that one, you fill your heart and mouth with gratitude as you go.

Attract Creative Traits

List the things that you would do if you knew the only outcome is victory. Select your top activity from that list and create small actionable goals that you can begin today. For example, if you want to be a leader, start examining how leaders think and act. You can read their biographies and apply some of the principles you learn right away.

Recommended Readings:

Who Moved My Cheese by Spencer Johnson

Make Today Count by John Maxwell

Listen:

You've Got To Be Hungry by Les Brown

Lord, thank You that You never sleep, You never slumber. Your eyes move to and fro in all the earth looking for those whose hearts are loyal; You want to show Yourself strong on our behalf. Mighty Lord, create in us clean hearts and give us pure hands as we want to be used in Your service but cannot without Your help. As we move in our assignments, we give You thanks that we are made whole. With grateful hearts, we pray in Jesus' Name and for God's sake. Amen.

(Hear + Do) Pray = Life

Note to Self

Day 15

Wellness

Dear Abba, there are times when I'm overwhelmed, I'm buffeted, and it seem as if I cannot take one more thing out of place. It is at these times that I seek You more, knowing that You have peace beyond my understanding, and it is well with my soul. Thank You, Lord.

Baseline: John 4:4-29

We see Jesus being targeted by the Pharisees once again (see John 4:1-3). This time He chose not to engage them but went in search of someone else who needed His attention. Here we come to a well-known story of Jesus meeting the Samaritan woman. I want to focus on her, her disqualification, and the equalizer. In the days of this story setting, people would go to the well in groups, usually for protection, and sometimes to help remove the stone which covered the well.

Here, the woman outside of the welcoming society comes to the well when most people would be away. It seems a bit similar to our time during the height of the COVID-19 pandemic where we have to observe social distancing and self-quarantine, some of us even to more extreme within our homes and away from the rest of the family. They are only allowed to the 'well' i.e., supermarket at certain times and in a certain order. I can imagine that as this woman made her way across town, mothers hastened their well-trained daughters inside because they saw this woman as contaminated and didn't want to associate with her.

It is ironic that the very thing that caused her to be isolated was the thing that created an opportunity for her to be with Jesus. Like the Pharisees, she was also religious. She knew where she should worship, and she even tried to impose the same social distancing on Him that had been placed on her. Jesus piqued her interest with a vision of not becoming thirty again. Maybe it appealed to her because she would no longer need to walk through the village to this well at this time of day, especially since it magnified her isolation. Sometimes it is the thing that we long for the most that Jesus uses to pull us to Him.

I must tell you that once you start to talk with Christ, it changes your life. One may question the logic which led from asking someone for water to getting into someone's personal life. I have heard that Christ is a gentleman; He will ask permission to come into your life; He stands at the door and knocks. Once you have opened the door, however, He uses the opportunity to fix all the things that need attention. So, this woman was able to get into a close relationship with Christ, something that being isolated made all the more possible. Maybe she would have been self-conscious to address the things that haunted her in a crowd, but up close and alone with Him, He allowed her to address what made her the subject of malicious conversation among others.

The great thing is that once she was filled with the living water, she ran to the very place where she had not been welcomed and invited them to share in the transformation she now experienced. Some would have still been judgmental if all she said was "Come see a man." The fact that she explained that He had revealed her truth, which she now openly discussed, created their capacity to believe.

Attract Creative Traits

In order to help others, you have to first address the issues you are facing. Examine the areas in your life that have caused you to be isolated. It may be an issue that you are not able to discuss with those closest to you. Use the time alone to bring it to Jesus. One way is to journal your thoughts on the issue, find scriptures that line up with it and allow God to show you how to move.

Recommended Readings:
Jesus Calling by Sarah Young

(Un)qualified by Steven Furtick

Poem:
Ain't I A Woman? by Sojourner Truth

Lord, I have many scars, some of which are from self-inflicted wounds. I have many times created situations that isolated me from others. But, Lord, I thank You that You give beauty for ashes, that You turn my mourning into dancing. Lord, the very thing that was meant to destroy me, You have used to bring others running to You so they never thirst again. Please fill my cup, Lord, let it overflow, and use me, Lord, Your humble servant. This I pray, in Jesus' Name and for God's sake. Amen.

(Hear + Do) Pray = Life

Note to Self

____

____

____

____

____

____

____

____

____

____

____

____

____

____

Day 16

The Shepherd's Gift

Abba, thank You for an abundant life. Thank You that as I get to know You more and my soul prospers, so does my life and the works of my hands. I do not fear evil because You are with me. Keep Your hands upon me, in Jesus' Name I pray. Amen.

Baseline: John 10:10

"The thief comes only to steal, kill and destroy: I have come that they might have life, and have it to the full." (NIV).

The Gospel according to John is different from the other three, which I call the tri-gospels. I believe his point of view was based on his proximity to Christ. In many cases, John refers to himself as the one whom Christ loves. He spent much of his time close to Jesus and this is remarkable as he was the youngest, based on conclusions made about his life. He outlived all the other disciples and is said to have lived to be about ninety-three years old.

In chapter 10, he spoke of the shepherd and the role that the sheep play. He also explained that there would be those who come in looking and acting like the shepherd but did not use the correct entrance. He paints this picture, and it would be consistent with the role that the shepherd plays in the life of the sheep during the time period. After a day in the pasture or walking across land, the sheep would go into an enclosure. This is usually a walled area with only one door. All the shepherds would leave their sheep with one shepherd on the watch that night. His only method of keeping the sheep in was laying across the door. When the other shepherds returned in the morning, each needed only to stand in the door and call out and only his sheep would come out. I find this fascinating. Can you imagine the joy we would experience if the only voice we respond to was that of our Shepherd, Jesus the Christ?

Like us, the sheep hear other voices as well, but they do not respond. Today, we are overwhelmed by so many voices: our own, the people around us, the media, and that of the enemy. In this season, it is important to know whose voice you follow. Attending to the enemy's voice is deadly. He comes to steal; he takes a little at a time, sometimes these things may even go unnoticed until there is a need for them. When we look around, something is missing; it may be a missed appointment, lost time or opportunity or money misspent. At first, it may not seem like much and, after all, we believe that we can gather more. As these small things add up, he kills parts of the individual who had an accumulation of missing things. It may be in the form of joy, a place to live, sleep or proper eating habits. Some of these lead to the destruction of the family, dreams, financial ruin, illnesses, and mental distraught. All this starts with listening to and entertaining the wrong voice. As we become like sheep, we must be very vigilant in protecting our ear gate as faith comes by hearing.

How can we learn to recognize the voice of the Good Shepherd? We must spend time with Him. The shepherd is generally alone with his sheep for most of its life. Therefore, spending alone time with God is critical if one wants to live a victorious life, and we must spend time in His WORD. Spending time alone with God affords us the opportunity to get to know Him intimately and obtain abundant life. It also gives us the valuable qualities needed to be successful in our everyday lives.

Attract Creative Traits

Evaluate the amount of quality time you spend in God's Word. Pray before reading and ask God for direction and understanding as you read. Keep a journal with you to record what He reveals to you about Himself, your life, and your world. Use these as part of your prayer focus.

Recommended Reading:

Fresh-Brewed Life by Nicole Johnson

Father, I know You hear us when we pray. Teach us to hear You when we pray. Let us understand that this is a two-way conversation, and not just us talking and putting in requests.

Help us to carve out time to spend with You. To be still and quiet before You so you can direct our paths. We are Your people and the sheep of Your pasture. With submitted spirits we pray, in Jesus' Name and for God's sake. Amen.

(Hear + Do) Pray = Life

Note to Self

Day 17

Witness Protection

Abba, thank You for those people who have paved the way before me. People who have fought for civil rights, educational equity, and the rights of a nation to have self-rule. In Your Word, You have blessed us with stories of giants who trusted You and came out victorious. Today, Lord, let me remember that You are with me as I press toward the mark of a higher calling in Christ.

Baseline: Hebrews 12:1-2

The book of Hebrews is thought to have been written by Paul the Apostle. It seems to "address a group of Christians whose faith was faltering because of the strong Jewish influences" (Encyclopedia Britannica). One of the most quoted chapters is the 11th where the writer speaks of faith. In that chapter, the writer sets us for a fantastic roll call. We get a glimpse into the lives of the greats like Abraham and Sarah, Moses and Joseph, Isaac and Samson. The record is presented of those people who overturned kingdoms and made justice work through their acts of faith (see Hebrews 11:33).

It is shown that they believed in God about their promises and actively worked to obtain them. They faced all kinds of circumstances and yet they were victorious. Their lives, while being lived, were not always attractive as they were at times homeless, in prison, without resources, and barren. Yet they believed and had their stories recorded. Hebrews 11:38 states that the world did not deserve them, but they made their way as best as they could on the cruel edges of this world.

These people lived extraordinary lives of faith but did not get their hands on the promises that God gave them. This fact does not seem to make sense until you see what comes out of it. Just take one person: Abraham. The promise to Abraham was that from him would come a great nation. To an old man with no children and an equally old wife, this was pure madness, yet in 2018 the Berman Jewish DataBank recorded over 14 million people in the core Jewish population, simply because this old man without children believed he would be the father of many. Consider Noah building an ark to protect against something they had never heard of before: rain, but was able to save his family. Now, why were their stories included and we are told that they did not even obtain their goals while alive? Is it possible that God has a better plan? That their faith would be the foundation for ours and complete the plan of God for our lives? Their stories are incomplete without ours.

So now that we have this great cloud of witnesses cheering us on, you go, girl, with your bad self. Grandma, read your Bible and pray for your child like your life depends on it and be the life of the whole house. Young lady, kick down those doors that illegally lock you out. Young man, fight hard for your dreams. If you don't immediately see yourself on this page, remember that they are cheering you on too! You, yes you, so you better win. Shed the extra weight and start running. Look to Jesus who started this race and completed His leg. He kept His eyes on the target and would not let up. Let us do the same, knowing we can.

Attract Creative Traits

Consider your life and the things you have accomplished so far. Examine the greater things that are pulling at you. What is something you dream of doing but it requires faith? Write it out and see how you can get it done a bit at a time. Before you are done, it may evolve into so much more than you know. One of my faith dreams is opening schools around the world. I will get them done too. Start working on yours today.

Father, I thank You for this witness protection program. It has kept my dreams alive when I would have given up a long time ago. When I think of Joseph and consider what may have gone through his mind while he was in prison and I saw Your hand when the time came, he was ready. I dust off the cobwebs from my dreams and I shine them up. I run with patience, a whole lot of speed and urgency, and total reliance on You. I am a witness for others too; they will see Your work in my life and glorify the Lord. Thank You for being a witness, in Jesus' Name and for God's sake. Amen.

Note to Self

Day 18

Being Willing To Be Led

Abba, You gave humans a great gift called choice. At times we use this to go our own way. Today, Lord, I lay my will down at Your feet. There will be times I want to take it up again, but that is the beauty of Your gift. Help me, Lord, to always use my gift of choice to please You. Thank You, Abba.

Baseline: **Psalm 23:2:**

"He makes me to lie down in green pastures; He leads me beside the still waters." (NKJV).

David is said to be a man after God's own heart. He knows what being a shepherd is like as he spent most of his early days in the field with the sheep. David recognized that the sheep without a shepherd gets into trouble. It is said that the sheep has a small brain, so it does not think much and so gets into trouble too much for itself. The shepherd usually carries a stick with a hook on its end and uses this to pull the sheep out of danger.

In Psalm 23, we see David reversing roles and now becoming the sheep. He recognizes that he gets into trouble and the Lord pulls him to safety. He finds himself in a wide-open space that is safe. It is filled with all the things he needs to flourish in a green pasture. This green pasture translates to many things for us today: a secure home, income to cover our expenses and have much leftover, a happy and joyful life. David is not just consuming but he is enjoying; he lies down in the pasture and has peace from his predators.

The Shepherd also leads him beside still waters. This sounds wonderful and calming until you consider the phrase "a silent river runs deep." So, the Lord may take you to a source that is so rich, has great depth and great potential but we have to rely on His leadership, lest the very thing He gives us consumes us.

Often when we are confronted with the issues of life, we read verse four: "Yea, though I walk through the valley of the shadow of death, I will fear no evil." (KJV). Let us examine this verse. Many times, we want the protection of the Shepherd but we are not willing to walk where He leads: the valley of the shadow of death. This is that thing that comes to take life from you, but you cannot skirt it, you have to go through it. As you go, you must have faith that He leads you. Today, many people look at sheep and refuse to be like them. While we admire and aspire to be lions, daring to be a sheep to the master Shepherd is equally important. What brave moves in valleys and still waters will we conquer and reap the benefits of when we are willing to submit to His leadership.

1. Become a great student. Be willing to learn then do.

2. Find yourself in God's Word. Read about David's life, his challenges, and his victories. Find other men and women who learned to live lives directed by their purposes.

3. Pray for the attribute of submission to godly authority, to your purpose, to God's plans for you.

Recommended Readings:

A Purpose Driven Life: What On Earth Am I Here For? by Rick Warren

The Threshing Floor by Juanita Bynum

Song:

Where He Leads Me I Will Follow by The Oak Ridge Boys

Father, thank You for leading me. In You I find that when the waters are deep, You sustain me. There are times in the valley of the shadow of death I am totally unaware of evil. You protect me from dangers seen and unseen. Good Shepherd, You take care of Your sheep and lead us into green pastures, areas of sustainability. We prosper because we rely on You, our Lord, our righteousness. Thank You, Lord, for Your guidance, as always, we pray in Jesus' name and for God's sake.

Note to Self

Day 19

At All Cost ~ Harriet Tubman

Abba, we thank You that we are fearfully and wonderfully made. Some people may look down on us because of what we look like or what we represent. This day, Lord, I worship You in the beauty of holiness, and I thank You that you give beauty for ashes. I dare to draw joy out of Your well of salvation. With this, I proclaim that it is well. Thank You, Abba.

Baseline: Luke 22:32

"...and when thou art converted, strengthen thy brethren." (KJV).

We spend time looking at the life of Harriet Tubman during Black History celebrations, but did we ever stop to really consider what she did? I think of Jesus speaking to Peter. He relayed how the devil, even Satan, had come to Jesus and asked for Peter. This means that Peter ranked very high in the spiritual world. It was clear that Peter was unaware of his status. While we are growing in Christ, we may be unaware of the gifts that we have. The enemy, however, can see those gifts and will try to sweep in and tear us apart. We can rest assured that Jesus has prayed for us and continues to make petitions for us before the Father. Each of us has the responsibility, however, to do our part. When we experience our change, we must bring that change to others.

When Harriet experienced freedom, she used her liberty to bring others to freedom. I find it electrifying that someone would risk death for others on so many occasions. Harriet's actions took a special type of courage and personal conviction about what she was facing. I think of some situations that I have left behind and said I would never go back to again. I now wonder, if I am asked to go back to get others out, if I would be willing to lay down my life so that others can be free. I use myself instead of we or us because this calls for personal decisions.

Harriet was so convinced about what she was doing that she was willing to kill anyone who started the journey and decided to back out. Are we willing to hold ourselves to such standards that we cannot compromise our values or the mission God has given us? There are weapons that we must use to help us fight. Are we familiar with the weapons of our warfare? Are they battle-ready and have we been using them? Are we using our praise and testimony (not telling personal business) to rescue others? Are you willing to pray without ceasing for a neighbor's child, even that neighbor with whom you disagree? Do you give of your time, money, blood, sweat, tears, and other resources to help ensure that others enjoy the freedom you do today? Consider how you can help others gain freedom.

Attract Creative Traits

1. Consider a situation that you have mastered. How can you offer your service or time to others facing the same situation?

2. To what extent would you go to help others who have started a journey to freedom? What would be your non-negotiable terms, and how would you implement them?

Recommended Readings:

Change Your Thinking Change Your Life by Brian Tracy

177 Mental Toughness Secrets Of The World-Class by Steve Siebold

Visit:

Rick Pina Faith & Patience Series ~ YouTube

Volunteer:

BASICS International (http://www.basicsinternational.org)

Your local church/community

In your home

Song:

Through The Fire by Hawk Nelson

Father, You have done so much for me, and You have carried me a far way. Now, Lord, You have given me the opportunity to give back. It is not always easy, and I may have to pay my own way. Some of the people I'm called to help refuse to get the help they need to change their circumstances. Yet I pray to be instant in season and out of season, to stand up to dogma, ridicule, and injustice. Thank You for sending help along the way, even from seemingly unlikely sources. I bless Your name who has given me witty inventions and taught my hands to war, in the mighty name of Jesus and for God's sake. Amen.

(Hear + Do) Pray = Life

Note to Self

____

____

____

____

____

____

____

____

____

____

Day 20

Cindy Trimm, Modern Woman Evangelist

Abba, thank You for this day. You have blessed me to be a blessing. Thank You for providing leaders in my generation who serve Your purpose. Help me to fulfill my purpose for this generation as well as leave a legacy for the ones to come. I humbly look to Your directions, in Your mighty name.

Baseline: John 5:39:

"…search the scriptures…" (NKJV).

"Today change ur attitude towards life according to Phil 4:8: Whatsoever things r true
Whatsoever things r honest whatsoever things r lovely whatsoever things r of good report, virtuous & praiseworthy I think on these things" ~ tweet@cindytrimm June 30, 2020

I met this woman of prayer on YouTube. I was growing in prayer when I found "Atomic Prayer." I had never heard someone pray like that before. What was more, she used the Word to fuel this prayer. Some phrases I didn't even know were in the Bible, such as asking for "witty inventions" (see Proverbs 8:12).

Based on her story, she used the Word of God to change her life. I can always imagine her as a young lady sitting up late at night, drinking in the Word of God. It reminded me of when I was growing up and studying for Bible challenges. This, by the way, set the stage for my love of the Old Testament. Cindy's story caused me to pay closer examination of my journey as a Christian. Not only do we need to read the Word of God, but we must also apply it. How can this change our lives? How can we breathe life in our dead places?

Recently I have been reading her book "The Art of War." It totally revolutionized the way I see prayer and spiritual warfare. We must recognize that we are at war, the war for our souls, lives, purpose, and future. It is not enough for me to simply pray prayers like I have a genie willing to grant me wishes. I must know the type of war I am in and work at being stronger in this battle. We sing of being overcomers but what are we overcoming? I looked back at things I wanted to achieve such as writing this book and was able to overcome using the weapon of prayer to gain a breakthrough.

"Bold Moves: Attract Creative Traits" helped me in such a magnificent way that as I wrote, my courage grew. Ideas developed that were not there at the beginning. I was attracting creative traits. Even meeting my deadline came with prayer. Each time I missed the mark, I went back in prayer. I learned about the Issachar's anointing, so I asked that I would walk in my right timing. I searched the scriptures for life in the situations I faced. I was deliberate in not sharing all I have learned about the stories of these bold movers as I want you to enjoy the benefits of searching the scriptures for yourself. As you look through the pages, stay awhile, eat up the Word and let it fuel you for the journey in making your own bold moves.

This was me attracting creative traits. I grew in areas not related to this book as well. That is the beauty of God. He wants to give us so much more. He sets the bush on fire to see if it would attract Moses. Today, He's doing the same thing to me and you. What has sparked your attention so that you must turn aside and look?

I challenge you to start this book again with new eyes. Invite someone along with you on this journey. It will change your life and the lives of those around you as it has done mine.

Attract Creative Traits

Prayer changes things. Learn how to pray effectively.

1. Find scriptures where people have prayed. Research the circumstances related to these prayers and the results. Document them so you can revisit them. More than all, study the Master of prayer, Jesus.

2. Write out scriptures related to your situation, good times and bad. Use these scriptures to formulate your prayers for these times.

3. Pray for guidance about what you should pray about.

4. Study other people who pray effectively, and do what they do until you have found your own breakthrough.

Recommended Readings:

The Art Of War For Spiritual Battle by Cindy Trimm

The Lifestyle Of A Watchman by James Goll

Fasting by Derek Prince

Prayer by James Revie

Song:

I Wish Somebaddy Soul Woulda Ketch A Fiya by New World Son

Note to Self

____

____

____

____

____

____

Day 21

Greatness Within

Abba, thank You for this person seeking You today. You have touched both our lives in such a marvelous way. We desire to make ***bold moves*** *every day of our lives. With You, Lord, we can accomplish the plans You have for us. Thank You, Abba, for greater works.*

Baseline: Philippians 4:13 and Proverbs 4:5-9

I reserved this chapter for you. As you read all the pages and looked at the people highlighted, did you consider yourself? Bold moves are for each of us. As you act, you will attract creative traits. God's desire is that we prosper. We cannot sit by anymore and let life pass us by. I know you have tried many times and it just did not work. There are those of you who have worked all your life and now just want to relax. There are others who have been consistently winning and just want to continue doing the same. I want to challenge you as you would not have gotten to this page without putting yourself in some of these shoes.

What bold move would you make today? Not the ones people expect you to make but the one that is really on your heart. Find yourself in God's Word and listen; He speaks to us. Hear what His plan for your life is, and I dare you to be bold.

A. Develop an attitude of "I can," no matter what. When you are filled with the understanding that God supports you, you will begin to attract the things you need to win.

C. Creativity comes from your imagination. Spend some time dreaming. See vividly the things you desire and enquire of the Lord. He will let you know if you are on the right path. Write them clearly as Habakkuk instructed us and pray over them with a heart opened to God's plan.

T. Develop the traits or habits that make you win. It may not come overnight but once you get it, keep building on it. Once the student is ready, the teacher will be right there. Be willing to go back to school every day. Learn from people, places, and things. Be willing to work while it is day and multiply the talents that God has given you.

Attract Creative Traits

Today you attract your own creative traits. Write out a bold move you desire to make and the way you will pursue it.

Bold moves never end!

Father, thank You for each bold mover today. Some have read this book but many only know the dream You have placed in their hearts. Give us all we need to push beyond the limits we have set for ourselves; give us courage, strength, and faith. Lead us to the place in Your Word where we can learn about ourselves in You. Let us harness our gifts and talents so You can add to them for the glory of Your kingdom. We declare war on average, mediocre, and procrastination and seek forgiveness for unbelief. We proclaim that we walk by faith and work the works of Him who sent us during the day. So now unto Him who is able to do much more than we ask or imagine, according to His power that works in us, we give glory and honor forever. Lord, accept our gifts, in Jesus' name and for God's sake. Amen.

(Hear + Do) Pray = Life

Note to Self

___

___

___

___

___

___

___

About the Author

Otensia grew up in a learning environment having her mom and older sibling as educators, and church was also an integral part of her life. Memorizing Bible verses and studying for the summer Bible competitions helped to develop the author's love for the Old Testament. ***Bold Move*** was inspired by the desire to share some of the Bible stories that others around her had not heard of before. It was also an opportunity for the author to bring her faith alive. She had seen many people who could talk about the scriptures but did not live victorious lives. Otensia then wanted to match the life skills she had learned with lessons presented on the pages of the Bible.

As a coach and motivational speaker, she uses the themes of courage and faith to help others see the value of overcoming obstacles and gaining their desired outcomes. Her experience as an educator influenced the format of the lessons which are adaptable. People across faiths, industries, cultures, and ethnicities are able to use the strategies outlined in *Bold Move* to attain their desired outcome. The writing of this book inspired the creation of the author's devotional podcast *Bold Move With Otensia*, that is streamed across several social media platforms. It was also the time during which the department she supervised increased, and she obtained several promotions in her financial career. As she wrote the lessons and later presented the podcasts, her life began to demonstrate courage she did not even know existed.

www.ingramcontent.com/pod-product-compliance
Lightning Source LLC
LaVergne TN
LVHW010106110826
845155LV00028B/503

* 9 7 8 1 9 5 3 7 5 9 8 0 1 *